A.M. CONVERSATIONS
WITH THE FATHER

TRANSFORM THE HEART, MIND, AND SOUL

NITISHA SPRINGER-MOORE

Printed in the United States of America
First Printing, 2017

ISBN-13: 978-1546621782 (CreateSpace-Assigned)
Library of Congress Control Number: 1546621784

TABLE OF CONTENTS

DEDICATION

To "Love" that lasts forever and beyond—a love that is tangible, a love that searches for me in my darkness, a love greater than any other ever known, as demonstrated on the cross. Where on Earth can we find such a love when humanity cannot love so completely and forgivingly? My love today, tomorrow, and throughout eternity is to my savior, healer, peace, joy, lifter, interpreter of tears....

It will be to the giver of gifts (Greg, Azalea, and Aniyah) ...Thank you, Jesus, for your LOVE.

FOREWORD

Merriam-Webster defines prayer as "an address (a petition) to God or a god in word or thought" or an "earnest request or wish." Many often use prayer as a way to center the self. Prayer changed my life. My definition of prayer is, "a discipline of seeking, connecting, and yielding to God," which I learned over time. I began with nothing more than a desire to end the constant pain I was in and to see changes in my life. I came to God broken and emerged whole and healed. Do not be fooled into thinking this is a journey at its end, but rather one that continues. I invite you into this journey with me because it works. God is real and He does answer prayers. To whom we direct our prayers is of utmost importance. As a Christian, I have positioned myself as a daughter under the teaching of Jesus Christ, instructed by what I consider my roadmap, the Bible. My prayer time spurred the title of this book, "A.M. Conversations with The Father." It is in testament to my time with God and how that time taught, challenged, and strengthened me. This book will outline the many lessons that I learned from my early morning experiences with God. It offers an intimate view of my brokenness, questions, pleas, discouragement, anger, obedience, disobedience, and breakthrough into healing, wholeness, and emotional and mental health as I began to experience a loving God. No matter what stage or season of life you are in as you enter into this new beginning, allow my transparency with God to lead you into your own revealing conversations with the Father.

"Father" is a title given to the creator of life, the sole place where our DNA originates. Yet, intimacy evolves as we stumble into unconditional love, a judgment-free experience that is kind, patient, consistent, and longsuffering. As you enter into prayer, seek with the objective to connect with the source of your being. He knows you. You are his. He longs for your intimacy. You are sought after. He understands you, and He loves you.

Here are my broken pieces

This journey began with a young woman who was abused sexually, emotionally, and mentally by her mother. The abuse of which I speak began at the tender age of six.

Below is a dialogue of the six-year-old in a twenty-year-old body:

With beads of tears coursing down her cheeks, and prayers pelting past her lips, "Why! Why! Why would you allow a little girl to experience such pain? Disgusted she asks who are you? I don't believe in you!" She sits, her heart filled with anger a single tear rolls down her cheek…

The heart of God spoke to mine as an unfamiliar, inner-knowing that flowed freely through my heart into my mental understanding and said:

There is no answer to the "why" that will ever satisfy you. The reason for which you seek an answer "is not important, the answer has arrived, I love you.

The words flowed from the unfamiliar voice, which I did not know then but later came to understand as the voice of God in my life. This created a hairline fracture in the frozen solid heart that weighed me down. During the next six months as I prayed, "I love you" was all that flowed into my heart and understanding. Slowly I yielded to this inner-knowing and offered my broken pieces one at a time for the next twenty years.

DAY ONE – LISTEN

On the first day, yearn and seek to identify the "unfamiliar inner-knowing" that flows through your heart and into your mental understanding. That is the voice of God speaking to your heart and introducing a foreign sound to your core. How does one know whether that voice is God or your own? God's inner-prompting is always in accordance with Scripture and Godly character. You can decide what time of the day is best, whether you are an early bird (like me) or a late owl, to quiet yourself, listen, sit, and pour out your heart.

My circumstances required pouring and emptying. They required the surrendering of pain, confusion, fear, anger, and lies in exchange for freedom. It is of utmost importance to open your heart and let it fly, for in God, you are in a safe place.

Why is this important? Does a doctor not look for a sterile environment free from possible contamination? Does a doctor perform surgery before cleaning the site of the wound? If not, such a practice could lead to infection, ultimately leading to death.

I have seen many devastated by struggles to live as persons of faith and then self-destruct. Self-destruction can occur when we do not allow the heart to empty itself out and thereby leaving blood trapped within. The presence of trapped blood in the heart is fatal. The purpose of the heart is to pump blood to various parts of the body—not hold it. If the heart retains blood, it causes a crisis in the body and affects all the other organs. When the heart can't bleed emotionally, maladaptive behaviors such as anger, un-forgiveness, depression, addiction, and even suicide begin to manifest. I have learned the importance of pulling away from the business of life and simply sitting, breathing, silencing the opposing voice, which is often mine, and collecting my thoughts from the realm of chaos to that of peace.

DAY TWO – THE INVITATION

"Come to me, all you who are weary and burdened, and I will give you rest." (Matthew 11:28). "Come to me," Jesus says. He is inviting you to come into a relationship with him. Jesus is saying to you, "Come to me, and I will give you rest." This is a promise made by God, for He alone can make such a promise. The promise states simply that if you come to Him, He will give you rest.

Coming to Jesus means entering into his presence. It means walking up to him in your mind and heart, exposing the truth of who you are and all you have done, and talking and sharing with him all that your heart holds. You might be thinking, "Oh, I can't do that—not with all that I am," but Jesus wants you just the way you are. Jesus does not put any restrictions on his invitation. He just wants you to come. Jesus says directly, "come," and he attaches a promise to it: "If you come, he will give you rest." The only condition to that promise is that you must come to him for him to fulfill his promise.

Jesus knows you, "All you who are weary and burdened." The fact is that Jesus already knows all about you. God made you and knows everything that you have ever thought or done. He knows your weaknesses and strengths, your ability to love, and your will to hate, and He loves you despite all these things, "Oh God, you know my foolishness; and my sins are not hidden from thee."

Jesus's love is unconditional. Jesus loves you just the way you are. However, he loves you too much to want you to remain unhappy and heavily laden with sin, troubles, bleeding hearts, and brokenness. In fact, this is why he is inviting you to come into a relationship with him. He knows only he can heal your wounds and give you strength anew to make your life joyful.

DAY THREE – THE PROBLEM WITH TRUST

"Choosing to make something important, vulnerable to another's actions…" --Brene Brown

Trust is both emotional and logical, which makes it one of the hardest things to do. Life has taught many of us that to trust is to give away our power. When we do that, we find ourselves in crisis. The interdependence needed for human social development is discomforting to say the least. Now, apply this understanding of trust to one of the most debated individuals in the world, Jesus. Trusting Jesus seems impossible from afar that is why he invites you to intimacy, closeness, and relationship. You are not expected to just hand over your vulnerabilities. Jesus walks with you through life and earns the right to your trust. I trust him now because he has proven himself to be trustworthy and faithful. What he has done for me has surpassed everything he promised at the beginning of my journey. Take a glimpse at where I began this journey with the Father: "I don't know how to trust God. I don't know how to begin to envision your love for me. What is this about? Why do you love me *now*? Did you not love me while I was being hurt? Show me who you are and why I need you! Help me to lean into you."

But now, O Jacob, listen to the LORD who created you. O Israel, the one who formed you says,

"Do not be afraid, for I have ransomed you. I have called you by name; you are mine. 2When you go through deep waters, I will be with you. When you go through rivers of difficulty, you will not drown. When you walk through the fire of oppression, you will not be burned up; the flames will not consume you. 3For I am the LORD, your God, the Holy One of Israel, your Savior. I gave Egypt as a ransom for your freedom; I gave Ethiopiaa and Seba in your place. 4Others were given in exchange for you. I traded their lives for yours because you are precious to me.

You are honored, and I love you. (Isaiah 43:1-3 NLT).

Do you know that you were called by name? That God called you into His creation and bestowed unto you gifts and talents to be explored? Are you going through a hard time or feeling like you are alone and God is not present in your reality? These verses explain how connected He is to you, and how much He loves you. You are specifically and uniquely called by name by the God of all creations. God knows *you*. God is neither afraid of your doubt nor afraid of your questions. He will extend Himself again and again until you know that He is real and that He is for you. That's mind-blowing!

Meditation

Meditate on the above scripture. Pray: "Father, I thank you for walking with me. Thank you for this time of intimacy and relationship with you. I will learn to trust you with my life, and I accept what you have allowed to occur in my life that has enabled me to develop. I trust that I will not always be where I am right now. This will make me into the person you created me to be. I rise now in my spirit, thinking, and emotions. Have your way. Show me You.

Questions

Father how do I become a vessel of your tangible love?

How do I lean into your love for me?

What does trusting you look like?

DAY FOUR – TRUST

The Greek word for trust is *Pisteuo*, to think to be true, to be persuaded of, to credit, or to place confidence in. It is ongoing work to trust Him. But there is a question that weighs in all our minds. How do I trust that which I cannot see? I cannot see God's current value with my finite mind. What is so unique about me and great about You that you would find me valuable? How is it that you could or would love me? Often this thought comes after life has dropped and broken us and left us with disappointments and failed expectations. The idea of a God who permits suffering is a deterrent to accepting Christ. The pain and confusion of one word—"why"—blinds us to the concept of Godly, unconditional love. This concept of love is distorted by our traumas. Like glass, we are shattered by a fall—the plunge that occurred when our expectations were not met. During that fall, we are cut by the broken edges of financial crises, failed marriage, toxic relationships, absent parents, abuses, emotional abandonment, domestic violence, and deaths of loved ones, along with other soul wrenching occurrences. Our vision lies before us, fragmented, after such cataclysms. Segments of our souls, identities, and self-images break. The composition of who we were is distant thought as we rise from the fall, camouflaged and determined to guard ourselves and keep such pain from ever happening again. A false sense of strength and distorted perspective are now the lenses we see through.

How have you changed?
I asked God: "Without a point of reference, how can one trust what cannot be seen or understood?" His answer: "One can be introduced and persuaded to trust, but, worse than not having a point of reference, is a trust experienced through the lens of brokenness.

Time with God provides the gift of sight. Being blind to my visual and mental distortion destroyed my internal happiness. I have learned that the moment we yield and give way to God's ideas and perspectives, He heals the darkness within. I will always remember one revelatory morning when God broke through the lies that were left in my heart. I wept, bitterly and without end, at the realization that my vision was killing me. I could not free my emotions because of my perspectives. I was giving my power away and victimizing myself, and I, who most deserved freedom, remained stuck while I was suffering! Had I not done that long enough at the hands of others? It was time for a change, so I accepted grace. Giving Jesus my hand was a choice to change the narrative of my life. Give God your hand and re-write your life story. Trust Him!

Meditation

What is man, that thou art mindful of him? And the son of man, that thou visits him? (Psalm 8:4 KJV).

The LORD gives sight to the blind, the LORD lifts up those who are bowed down, the LORD loves the righteous (Psalm 146:8 NIV).

Opening yourself to God creates room for visitation. The truth in God's word gives sight to the blind!

Questions

What and when was the "fall"?
What did that "fall" shift in you?
What is the health of your vision?
What/who do you trust in?

DAY FIVE – Fear

When I stop, time stands still, and silence floods me. My smile turns to tears, and my tough skin gives way to a broken heart. My strong mind is invaded with self-doubt, my independence turns needy, and my mask fades when I pause. That fear, which haunts and blocks me from the life God died to give me, suddenly rushes in. I tell myself, "the devil is a liar!" but is the liar really the devil or is it *me* as I am being confronted by my past? The plaguing question remains, "God, why does it still hurt after I have been delivered and set free from my past?"

I am haunted by what wasn't, what should have been, and consumed with "whys" in the silent pause as I fight to keep the tears from escaping my eyes. I tell myself positive words, but they come undone in the silence of truth. I keep it moving, afraid to stop, and afraid to face the reflection that is me. To stop is inevitable. I search, looking deeper, and suddenly I see a champion in my reflection, not because of my victories, but rather because the storms in life have not overtaken me.

Forging ahead and led by the voice of Jesus, when I pause in the silence, I feel God's unconditional love gently removing the mask. I am faced with all that makes me, me. My spirit tells a story that my mind cannot comprehend—the tales of my mistakes, failures, valleys, triumphs, victories, mountain tops, and struggles working together for my good. Now when I stop, the rule of fear is defeated. I submit to Him who causes me to rise above it all, whose love never fails, and who sees into my destiny and proclaims from my beginning to my end, "you win!"

Meditation
I, the LORD, have called you to demonstrate my righteousness. I will take you by the hand and guard you, and I will give you to my people, Israel, as a symbol of my covenant with them. And you will be a light to guide the nations (Isaiah 42:6 NLT).

But Jesus immediately said to them, "Take courage! It is I. Do not be afraid." (Matthew 14:2 NIV).

Questions

Can you relate to this poem?

Write your version of it.

When you are alone, still, and tuned into your heart, what plagues your mind?

DAY SIX – FEAR OF HOPE

The fear of hope is not usually outright discussed because in most cases, we do not know that it is hope that we are avoiding. Hope is not optimism. Optimism is having a positive perspective. It is defined as the degree to which a person believes that positive outcomes will occur rather than negative outcomes. Hope is a positive desire with expectation attached. A hopeful person believes specifically in his or her own capability to secure a successful and fulfilling future. For Christians, Jesus is our hope! Through the lens of faith, we grab hold of our greatest potential and determination to achieve successful fulfillment. It is hope in Jesus that summons the believer to prayer. Prayer gives us a vantage point from on high to look low. Prayer elevates our vision to look at life from heaven's panorama view. It is here that we are left with hope that all things are working together for our good, not just because the Bible tells us this but because we have allowed our hearts and minds to step outside of our reality and probe the mind of the designer of life, Jesus who has a plan for us all. Fear is the enemy to hope. It drowns and diminishes its brightness.

Here was my conversation with the Father: "Father, what if I open up the place of longing and desire within me to let myself feel deeply how much I want (what is your earnest, unspoken desire?) only to discover that those desires are not, or cannot be, met in your plan for me?" These subconscious thoughts sabotage and paralyze. As long as fear is governing our steps to freedom and discovery, we will give into the subtle lie that is attached to this mindset. Here is the Truth: "Trust in the Lord and do good; dwell in the land and enjoy safe pasture. Take delight in the Lord, and he will give you the desires of your heart. Commit your way to the Lord" (Psalm 37: 3-5 NIV). Check your heart. Is what you desire prompted by divine love? God promises to give you the desires of your heart. God's "NO" is protection from what you cannot see. Trust that. His "DON'T" can almost always end in, "hurt yourself." Do not hurt yourself!

Prayer: "I confess today that I am afraid to harbor hope. It is painful to hope. How will I live with desire that is awakened rather than repressed? What will I do with the disappointment? Can you sustain me? Are you enough for my thirst?" Such questions open the way for Christ to lead us into deeper levels of spiritual truth and healing. Today, hear the Father saying, "those who drink the water I give will never be thirsty again. It becomes a fresh, bubbling spring within them, giving them eternal life" (John 4:14 NLT).

Meditation:

Come and see a man who told me everything I ever did! Could he possibly be the Messiah? (John 4:29 NLT).

Today I encourage you to explore your repressed emotions and desires. It seems scary, right? It was for me too. Yet, it was on this very morning during my journey as I sanctioned my heart to break free in the safest place on earth—the presence of our creator—that the walls of my heart gave way. Healing was applied. It is God who stirs and beckons you to sit with Him. I invite you to come see a man who told me all about Nitisha.

Questions

What are your deepest desires?

Why are you afraid?

What is the worst that can happen if the answer is "no" or "wait?"

What do you see as you view life from heaven's perspective?

Father, you show up every time I need you, not according to my wants but according to your artistry. You are the artist of my design. When searching through life's memories, uncontrollable tears escape me as I remember that you have always shown up for me. During the darkest of nights, Lord, you are present. During the brightest of days, Lord, you are present. Your imprint is on every page of my life. Thank you for showing up for me!

DAY SEVEN – BREATH

What is in you that is causing difficulty? This fear, this challenge, this rejection, this...too shall pass but not before working for your good. Do you know that breath is not simply a sign of life but is also the sustainer of productivity? What can you produce if you cannot inhale or exhale? The adversary, either by subjective or objective means, aims to suffocate and stop production in your life. I cried out this morning, "help, I can't breathe! I am suffocating. Antagonistic murmuring, infliction, and cowardice are a hindrance and obstruction to my productivity. I am overwhelmed by life. The gifts you bestowed upon me have become unbearable weights, dragging me into despair. Father, grant me the strength to pull deep my courage and breathe through life with you as my primary source of air. Allow my body, mind, and soul to be transformed by the power of your breath. Just as life began by your breath, equip me to breathe life into all gifts in me.

Meditation

Therefore, since we have been justified by faith, we have peace with God through our Lord Jesus Christ. Through him we have also obtained access by faith into this grace in which we stand, and we rejoice in hope of the glory of God. Not only that, but we rejoice in our sufferings, knowing that suffering produces endurance, and endurance produces character, and character produces hope, and hope does not put us to shame, because God's love has been poured into our hearts through the Holy Spirit who has been given to us (Romans 3:1-5).

Consider trouble as a stimulant. Without it we would not be perfected, here perfected means mature. Just as water is purest when it is in motion, so are people generally strongest during times of affliction. The breath of God aids you to breathe through difficulty, disappointment, grief, and distress. I encourage you, who have been holding your breath, by reason of the void at the core of your existence, to breathe deeply, inhaling the fervor and avowal of God and exhaling frustration and doubt. Exchange your dilemma for God's grace to drive you forward. Breathe through it.

Questions
What is sapping your breath?
How does this scripture speak to you?

DAY EIGHT – STRENGTH

Understanding that God is the most significant being in your life is crucial. Choosing His will over your own gives you a confidence that is not easily expunged. Learning to comfortably survive seasons of little and to abound in strength. To choose silence when you wish to speak is wisdom. To choose discipline over emotion is maturity. To accept God's course of action and character over your own is growth. Be planted. No one takes your life—you willingly lay it down because that is what God models for us. Sacrificing, pushing forward, pressing deeper, and obedience to what God says has never failed me, and it will never fail you!

I know both how to be abased, and I know how to abound, everywhere and in all things, I am Instructed both to be full and to be hungry, both to abound and to suffer need. I can do all things through Christ which strengthened me (Philippians 4:12-13 KJV).

Meditation

Reconstruction of your heart requires various seasons. Not every season will feel good, but they are necessary parts of your process to wholeness. It hurts like hell, but when it is done, it is done.

Prayer

"Father, satisfy me in your word and surround me with your presence that I may endure each season as a committed soldier!"

Study

What is a good soldier?

What is the posture of a soldier?

What weapons do I have at my disposal?

DAY NINE – HE'S CALLING YOU

Father, am I unlovable? Why do those who are supposed to love me wound me? Father: "My precious creation, your focus is wrong. The people you seek love from are human. Prone to error, they are fighting their own internal battles. Those people do not have the capacity you require. I created you with unique complexities that life experiences have altered. Your worthiness is not determined by another's ability to love you. It is accepting that I alone am enough to fill your voids and love you completely. Time spent trying to please and earn love is wasted. Learning of Me and allowing Me to teach you how to love yourself as I love you quenches the soul's thirst. Revealing yourself to the world to bring to it the gift that is you is worth the process. Do not waste time."

Meditation

When Jesus heard him, he stopped and said, "Tell him to come here." So they called the blind man. "Cheer up," they said. "Come on, he's calling you!" (Mark 10:49 NLT). Did you know that while you cannot see what He is doing He is calling you forward? What narration are you reliving? Could it be that the narrative you are telling yourself is a lie? The inner voice reminding you of your fears and failures will always fight for dominance in your life. Tell yourself another story by listening for the only voice that matters: Jesus's. "He's calling you!"

Questions

What is Jesus saying to you in this moment?

What is the lie?

What is the truth?

DAY TEN – WORTHINESS

There are two main forces working against Jesus being the savior we need. The first is pride, which entails having a *superiority* complex and not accepting his invitation to change the condition of your heart. The second is an *inferiority* complex, which involves being self-absorbed, stuck in unworthiness, and entertaining the thought that God could not love you, thus leading you to refuse to accept His offer of love and salvation. Accept the gift of Jesus today. He gave his life for you. Your rejection of the love and peace of God, the refusal to seek Him and partake of His mercy which is freely given, and abhorring the contentment of His finished work on Calvary is just as arrogant as the one who says in his heart, "I am good, I don't need it." God's grace is given to us so that we might choose to walk worthy of our calling.

Prayer

"Father, I step back and let you step forward. Be in charge, Father. You see my ending. I surrender my future to you. My perception is skewed and eclipsed by the truth that I am driven by my sinful nature, therefore unloved by you. Please correct my choices, beliefs, thoughts, and perceptions, which have fed my suffering. I am willing to submit my perception to you that I might have spiritual insight. I choose you to be my guide. Amen."

Meditation

So we keep on praying for you, asking our God to enable you to live a life worthy of his call. May he give you the power to accomplish all the good things your faith prompts you to do. (2 (Thessalonians 1:11 NLT)

Action Item

Look into the mirror and affirm, "I deserve more because God died for me to have more!" I am worthy and deserving of love, joy, peace, and happiness.

Questions

Are you harboring inferiority or superiority complexes?

Accept today that what is "wrong" can only be corrected by God's power working in you and not your own.

What is your faith prompting you to do?

DAY ELEVEN – "THE BLEEDING FIGHTER"

Visualize with me if you would: Rocky is in the ring, face bloodied, the paces in his bounce have dwindled, and his punches are faint. The blows he has taken have visibly worn out this fighter. Yet the crowd is insistently yelling his name. Rocky is tired, yet fighting to remain standing, determined not to fall. Is this you? Have you repeatedly endured life's harshest hits? Have you grown weary as your light dimmed?

The Father offers you rest today. The issue with false Christianity is that it seems to encourage a type of superhuman behavior. This has caused many to walk away in defeat. I wanted to walk away! In fact, I had a plan. I was alone on a bus traveling from North Carolina back to my home in New York. While making a rest stop, I was contemplating getting off the bus and just walking away to become a new person with a new hair color, name, and identity—an identity that did not include being a Christian minister, speaker, mentor, or author. I just wanted to be free. The call to be our greatest selves comes with a price that is often left unspoken. It is a price every person called to greatness has paid. I have been a bleeding fighter for as long as I can remember. But the journey on which you have decided to join me by reading this book has kept me from bleeding out or bleeding on other people. I am committed to carrying my bloody heart to God every morning. He has been faithful in healing, teaching, strengthening, and loving me every morning, noon, and night. The Father sees our greatest stumbling block. His will is to consume us completely, sharpening every gift and talent by healing our inner being to stand alert and strong as more than a conqueror by resting in Him.

Meditation

You have been strong, and you have been an encouragement to many, but silently your heart bleeds. Be encouraged that this too is part of the process. Did you know that your blood speaks? Just as the blood of our Father speaks of his sacrifice and victory over death, your blood tells the story of your victory and reveals the glory of our savior. As you read, this is my blood speaking to your heart about the blood of Jesus that heals. Do not be afraid to bleed because it introduces you to the healer.

Questions

What is the condition of your heart?

Are you carrying your bloody heart to Jesus or are you hurting yourself and others?

Prayer

"Father, teach me how to fight so that I do not get weary in my well-doing." He sees you and He loves you!

There are no more worries about worth. There is no more emptiness caused by what is missing, no more waiting to live, no more expecting empty vessels to fill you. God is more than enough! His love for you never fades, fails, or disappoints. To know Jesus is to have found the greatest love of all. That love is in pursuit of *you*.

DAY TWELVE – LOVED

Internal suffering loses its power in the presence of God. The voices that dishonor, discourage, and disarm you lose their strength when surrounded by the love of Christ. Does it matter so much what does or does not happens externally when we have an internal stability? Refocus and live despite the voices! To be in love has been associated with words and phrases such as smitten, swept off your feet, or engulfed. While you are waiting and searching for that kind of love, allow me to draw your attention to unabridged, unconditional love that says I adore you as you are, controls the elements and humanity to show you your worth, knows your moods, and understands your properties. God does not mind being your savior. He will save you every time. He loves being your God. He loves the exchange of intimacy in worship. Hear Him now as he whispers, "I love you." Listen for the voice that tenderly engulfs you and loves you without hesitation. You are loved completely.

Meditation

LORD, you alone are my portion and my cup; you make my lot secure. The boundary lines have fallen for me in pleasant places; surely, I have a delightful inheritance. I will praise the LORD, who counsels me; even at night my heart instructs me. I keep my eyes always on the LORD. (Psalm 16:5-8 NIV).

With him by my right hand, I will not be shaken. Today there are no questions to study, but rather an affirmation to repeat until the tears flow, the hardness of your heart crumbles, and you know deep within that this is your new sense of being. On the morning that God instructed me to make this declaration, chains literally broke in and off my life. Let the flow of the Spirit leap off the pages of this book and break every chain in your life. Do not expect the worst any longer. Expect love in all things.

Affirmation

"I am Loved, I deserve Love, and I freely give Love. Therefore, I *expect* Love.

DAY THIRTEEN – THE POWER OF CHOICE

Today I choose to help others even if they don't ask for it. I choose to take care of myself. I choose to be around people who add to my life and give grace to those who don't deserve it. I choose to step out of my comfort zone and try new things as well as step out of the box and consistently evolve. My life will be in service to others. I will make time for my hobbies. I choose to forgive and search within myself when I am annoyed. During highs and lows, I remind myself that "this too shall pass." I refocus and apply energy toward the things I can control. Today I use my power of choice! Choices govern the direction of life. They govern outlooks, future plans, and my idea of success. Choose to walk this journey to the end, walk away from agitation, pain, neediness, and flight. Instead choose to let the heat reveal your brilliance and let it burn, setting ablaze the effects of yesterday so that you can walk forward with the Master to adequateness without scapegoats—just you and Jesus. I charge you, no matter how cold or how hot it gets, to endure. As you let it burn, rest assured that you are changing. Things that are not useful to your future are melting off of you. Love will find you the way you deserve it. Do the work.

Meditation

Make a choice for your life. Listen to the birds as they sing, see the flowers you often rush past without acknowledgment. Pause and take notice of God and His presence in your life. Begin to look for kisses from God. Looking through a lens of gratitude, see the hand of God shielding you and moving in your life. Smile! Today is a great day! So, dance to the rhythm of joy and sing to the beat of life. After all, you only get one life here on earth.

Questions

What must you allow to melt off of you?

Today, search for moments of laughter and call the friend that makes you laugh.

Use your power of choice to stay positive and righteous.

DAY FOURTEEN – BYE, HATER!

Have you ever felt strong and focused walking strong and then…trip! A trip on a crack is often caused by leaving a crack left unattended. This is a great opportunity for the hater within you to bring up your disgrace and deter your focus. The hater, more often than not, is you. Other times it is the enemy of our soul trying to bury us under condemnation. In recent readings, you have been encouraged to think strong and live mightily. Of course, the hater rises to remind you of the "real you." STOP! No, not today hater! Becoming acquainted with your pattern of behavior is crucial to emotional intelligence. The pattern of thoughts and behaviors toward which you are unconsciously pulled will shed light on your mental and emotional health. I realized that the first thoughts of my day were negative. The moment I opened my eyes, negative self-talk flooded my mental space.

Prayer is such an important space because removing yourself away from the noisiness of life allows you to self-evaluate. My prayer time was not simply praying for an answer. I was praying for an escape from myself. Prayer allowed me to constantly hear myself and become aware of the fear that was controlling me. Listen deeply to what you are asking and talking to God about. It reveals so much. I was listening to myself talk to God and I did not like what I was hearing over time. God is patient and kind. The answers that He gives will help you not only today, but will continue helping you for life. I am still thriving due to the answers I received in the first year of my journey. I am writing this book because everything that God has taught me has worked for me. It will work for you. You can be happy and free from emotional bondage and mental anguish.

Your Father lovingly reminds you that you are not the voices in your head or the external voices. You are favored with grace and mercy each new day. The trick of the enemy is to focus you on your condition rather than on the promises of God and a bright future. Do not be locked into emotional distress, mental anguish, and fears that come to steal your joy, vision, and peace. How can you live your best life and walk in the freedom to which God calls you if you are blinded by what you are not instead of focusing on who you are? Rise up in your spirit now! Begin to say aloud who you truly are. List those adjectives: dedicated, strong, loyal, fun, caring, kind, generous, etc.

Meditation

I have told you these things, so that in me you may have peace. In this world, you will have trouble. **But take heart! I have overcome the world.** (John 16:33).

You are walking with the best! Put on your cutest outfit today and show the world who rules! Show the world that this power in you has overcome the world. Go and get it today!

"Get what, Tish?"

Whatever you want that aligns with the Master's plan. Let's Go!

Questions

What is your basic, emotional, posture? Positive or negative, angry or fearful, joyful or sad, etc.?

What do you hear when you pray? Do you like it?

What has God revealed to you about you?

What truth is in God's word concerning you to defeat the lie?

DAY FIFTEEN – PERSONAL SUPPORT

Today as I studied David, one of my favorite Bible characters, I related to him in an amazing way. David writes Psalm 142 by pouring out his heart right from the start about his experience in the cave as described in 1 Samuel 22. David finds himself in a dark, lonely place, and he is overcome with disappointment. He looks around and sees no one there, which causes deep disappointment and hurt (Psalm 142:4). Why? Because he defeated the national threat, Goliath (1 Samuel 17)! Where were all the people for whom he risked his life? Have you ever wondered where all the people for whom you have loved, supported, and shown up are? David says that he looked around and saw a place void not of people, but of personal support, "no one is concerned about me, no one cares about me" (Psalm 142:4). Today I encourage you just as I have encouraged myself on many occasions. The Lord, Jesus Christ, cares about you and is concerned about you! Pour out your heart to him. He is waiting.

Meditation

He only is my rock and my salvation; He is my defense; I shall not be moved. In God is my salvation and my glory; the rock of my strength, and my refuge, is in God. Trust in Him at all times, you people; Pour out your heart before Him; God is a refuge for us. Surely men of low degree are a vapor, men of high degree are a lie; If they are weighed on the scales, they are altogether lighter than vapor (Psalm 62:6-9 NKJV).

Questions

Who are you expecting to support you?

What if they never support you?

Prayer: "Father, help me to reach for your unfailing hand."

DAY SIXTEEN – I AM THE BRAVEST PERSON I HAVE EVER MET!

Today I woke up with a broken heart about things in my life that I have chosen to endure in an effort to be like Christ. As I pour my heart out before Jesus, I hear in my spirit, "Who told you, that you had to do this to be like me? I asked you to stand still so that I could perfect the masterpiece that was tarnished by allowing rejection, negligence, and isolation to rub against wounds that controlled you. This is now your choice! I have taught you about worth and proven by my provision that you are worth everything. I have taught you that you are stronger than every weapon fashioned and leashed against you. I have shown you through trials that you are strength! Move forward, my daughter, in wholeness, making decisions from a place of transformation. When you do, standing tall will not feel like frailty but rather a display of a power greater than your own. The father boldly states, "For that which I have established cannot be undone!" Understanding this proclamation lifts you higher than any opposition you face. With fearlessness, you can walk in the attributes of your Father: boldness, mercy, kindness, love, compassion, and grace. For his word goes before you!

"Heaven and earth will pass away, but my words will never pass away" (Mark 13:31 NIV).

Meditation

Learn the lesson. Endure the suffering that accompanies the process of becoming a better you, but please do not suffer longer than you must! You can stand still and be transformed from victim to victor in your mind, heart and soul.

Questions

What am I sitting in that is old, history, past, or overdue?

What is it accomplishing in me?

Father, help me to remember that you established me and I cannot be undone!

Waiting is difficult and can result in emotional, mental, and even physical chaos. The waiting season produces visions that reveal possibility, and a voice that whispers hope, which the natural mind doubts, questioning its validity. This paradox contributes greatly to the difficulty of waiting on God. Be encouraged today that your steadfast focus on the vast greatness of our God is worth life's seasons of waiting. The manifestation is closer than you think. Hold on

DAY SEVENTEEN – DISAPPOINTMENT SUCKS!

Have you ever expected to get an orange but got a grapefruit instead? Have you ever wanted something sweet but received something bitter? You start looking around for the cameraman to jump out and say, "Punked!"? What about crossed a sea of obstacles just to find yourself dying of thirst in a desert?

These accounts confirm that disappointment is a necessary for securing true, inner joy. Human tenacity is such that when we have nothing to pull from externally, we turn within to search for deeper meaning. So, we smile at the rise and setting of the sun. We recognize the beauty in laughter and find joy. We may miss out if we allow ourselves to stay stuck in painful places of disappointment and refuse this precious three-letter word: "joy." If our eyes are filled with self-pity, we miss the moments of glory that await us. Open your eyes. There is life to live and it is filled with wonder. Disappointment is a place we journey through on our way to joy, not a place of lodging. When we become spiritual, the focus on self-preservation diminishes and truth becomes the goal. Beware of your emotions as they can drive you either to seek God or further from God. Emotions do not authenticate truth, but they do authenticate our understanding of truth.

Meditation
These things I have spoken to you, that my joy may be in you, and that your joy may be full. (John 15:11 NKJV).

Questions
How has disappointment paralyzed you?

What has the spirit revealed about your emotional state?

What has your heart spoken?

DAY EIGHTEEN – PIECES OF MY HEART!

This morning, clenching my hands on my chest as I bend over in agony, I cry out, "my heart, Father, I do not want this heart! Here is my heart, Lord—the one you gave me that is purely overtaken by love and good intentions yet, at times, is trampled on. I yield it to you, Lord, so that it will continue to beat to your rhythm and in time with your call for my life to love, not as this world understands love, but as you have displayed it. Father, because it is yours, you know this heart, which at times aches from injustice, unwarranted actions, and carelessness, that has encouraged and cried on behalf of others, but is has also been rejected. God, take your heart, which I have broken, rejected, and denied and fight for me! I yield this bloody, fragile heart to you.

Have you ever felt this way? Has your heart been so badly wounded that physical pain is present?

Meditation

My flesh and my heart may fail, but God is the strength of my heart and my portion forever (Psalm 73:26 NIV).

God comforts the broken hearted.

Questions

What does a heart of God look like?

How are you protecting your heart?

DAY NINETEEN – EVIDENCE OF MY PRIVATE COMMITMENT

Father, as I begin this day, may I feel your presence, walk in power, love freely, forgive quickly, smile brighter, encourage many, and die to myself. Make me more like you. Lord, help me exude brightly your glory through my actions and deeds. Help me to bring my mind into oneness with You. The world needs You. Use me as your reflection. As I die, may you rise!

Meditation

22 But the fruit of the Spirit is love, joy, peace, forbearance, kindness, goodness, faithfulness, 23 gentleness and self-control. Against such things there is no law. 24 Those who belong to Christ Jesus have crucified the flesh with its passions and desires. 25 Since we live by the Spirit, let us keep in step with the Spirit. (Galatians 5:22-25 NIV)

Questions

What does it mean to be more like you?

Which "fruit" are people walking away with after an encounter with me?

What can I do to "crucify" my flesh?

This is a continuous prayer and discipline. They will not be achieved and finished. We will always revisit this page.

DAY TWENTY – I THIRST

Today I am fully aware of my humanity. I feel the longing to give into my desires and quench the thirst that is within me. What do I do with these feelings, Father? How do I overcome that which pulls me further from you? How do I stand on weak legs? How do I live in this dry place? This day I cry out and lay my humanity before you so that you might transform my fragility into supernatural strength. Help me avoid the traps that await and intend to derail me. Thank you for leaving me the comforter, your Spirit, which leads and guides me. Give me the courage to be obedient. Help me to choose Your will over my own today. I submit to you and I let this flesh burn until it dies. I submit to you as Lord over my life, and I trust that you will withhold no good thing from me. I accept the truth that you alone are enough for me. Satisfy me now. In Jesus's name. Amen.

Meditation

The LORD will guide you always; he will satisfy your needs in a sun-scorched land and will strengthen your frame. You will be like a well-watered garden, like a spring whose waters never fail (Isaiah 58:11).

Questions

What do you hear the Father saying?

What am I longing for?

Why do I continue to desire this?

Will it satisfy me or leave a larger void?

DAY TWENTY ONE – CRAFTILY BROKEN

You were Craftily broken for this moment of strength. Today, praise God for freedom. I do not need what I needed yesterday. I found out that some of what I needed stemmed from past, negative experiences. This relationship with God is all I have ever needed to fill the void. There is no human in existence that can fill me so completely. I appreciate family and friends who love me and touch my heart to the best of their ability. They make my life experiences joyful, but they simply are not God. As I obey, I become healed. I become wiser as I seek wisdom, knowledge, and understanding. I am made free as I trust him completely, and the more I learn of him, the more I learn about me. You were not just broken but rather your life has been crafted by the hand of God to become His masterpiece. The price of becoming the person you were created to be will be expensive, but you are fine and you are going to make it. You are in the hands of God. Replace the tears of your heart with trust. God is in control, and He knows what He is doing.

Meditation

Before I formed you in the womb I knew you, before you were born I set you apart; I appointed you as a prophet to the nations (Jeremiah 1:5).

Questions

Father, show me the beauty of my brokenness.

Help me to trust you.

How can I use my experiences to help others?

Make me unashamed of my experiences, knowing they were not for me alone.

The moment you set your will to accomplish a task is the moment an attack is launched. The test is to believe that God can help you against all odds and will help you to overcome. To live out our favorite worship song in the valley reveals the depth of our roots in God. Self-preservation will always be in opposition to sacrifice. Be encouraged today and know that God will honor your sacrifice. Choosing His will above your own will bring about the greatest manifestation of His power and glory in your life.

DAY TWENTY TWO – FAITH THAT IS OUT OF THIS WORLD

I asked God a question, "What is it about me that you love more than everyone else?" When I think back now at that question, it seems ridiculous. In that moment, I was feeling the inclusivity that comes with a personal relationship with Jesus Christ. What has caused my evolution is the way my humanity asks infantile questions to a magnanimous God. God not only answers the question but also provides wisdom, knowledge, and understanding. The response I received has fed me continually and shaped my understanding of infinite versus finite. God replied to me, "What is it that makes you think I love you more than all of my creation? Your system of measurement could never be used with me. Man's mind simply cannot comprehend my depth. I give to you from myself just as I give to all of my children. What I have given you is your portion of grace. Never look at another's grace and judge it. You don't understand it. How could you?" "Because of the privilege and authority God has given me, I give each of you this warning: Don't think you are better than you really are. Be honest in your evaluation of yourselves, measuring yourselves by the faith God has given us" (Romans12:3 NLT).

Meditation

Faith that lives outside of reason will not be understood by humanity How can the limited mind of man grasp it? To this world your faith will not make sense. Please remember that God is too great to fit into our system of measurement and reason. For this reason, we walk by faith and not by sight. Have you restrained and limited God by believing that His goodness is based on results? Our discontent is often fueled by the results we expect.

Questions

How are you measuring your life?

Are you discontented? Why?

Are you missing the power of your portion of grace? Faith moves mountains.

DAY TWENTY THREE – YOU ARE ENOUGH

Why focus on that which is temporary when there is greater work and a greater call to action? Take your eyes off of your problems and analyze the bigger picture. Ask yourself, "Why do I continue to be entangled in this mindset?" In a small but powerful whisper, hear the Father beckoning you to abandon this reoccurring mindset, which steals time. Individuals are waiting for *you* to tell them about how God has shown up during the difficulties in your life, not just your Sunday morning experiences when you are looking good, acting right, and following a "love our neighbor" type of Christianity. Share the times that you felt lost or failed and God did not condemn you. Share times when, instead of judgment, you received great compassion. God blesses during moments when we deserve punishment. Share the stories about when your mind was confused due to your circumstances, and God provided clarity and hope. Tell how he met you at the place of despair and led you safely out of it into sanity. Tell the world about the One who has never left your side. That is good news!

Meditation
For God has not given us a spirit of fear and timidity, but of power, love, and self-discipline (2 Timothy 1:7 NLT).

Questions
The next time you feel sorry for yourself, lapse into self-pity or feel inadequate, ask yourself:
"Where do these feelings come from?"
Do they connect to a feeling of not being enough, do you not trust your choices, or are you feeling misunderstood and unappreciated?
Work through these by surrendering your truth to God.

DAY TWENTY FOUR – ROYALTY

As we mature, we understand the importance of our voices. Do not lend your voice to that which is wasteful. Protect your way of thinking by connecting daily to the frequency of heaven. As a result, your speech will change. Knowing who you are makes you aware of the weight your words carry. Should a king or queen be careless with their words? No. Because when they speak, things happen, there are real consequences. Such is your position in the kingdom of heaven as an ambassador of Jesus on earth. Your tongue carries power! It carries the power of life and death. You are entrusted with the power of heaven so, use it. Speak the words of heaven. God watches over His word to perform it (Jeremiah 1:12 NIV).

Meditation

Even fools are thought wise if they keep silent, and discerning if they hold their tongues. (Proverbs 17 NIV)

Questions

How will you restrain your thoughts and therefore your words?

For a week, consider your words closely. What are you saying?

What do your words reveal about the way you think?

How are you watering your future self?

DAY TWENTY FIVE – AFTER EFFECTS

My prayer this morning: "Father, I am in constant emotional pain. What is wrong with me? Is it my husband? Is it my children? Is it my financial situation? Is it dissatisfaction with my living environment? Why am I living in pain?"

The phrase "emotional sensitivity" dropped into my spirit. Through the study of self, I found that emotional sensitivity means experiencing emotions at a higher intensity than most people. The results are constant discomfort, distress, and suffering. There are too many emotions to manage. Emotions hit hard and are difficult to control. Why does this happen? Sexual abuse affects children and adults across ethnic, socioeconomic, educational, religious, and regional lines. According to childtrauma.org, in the United States, one out of three females and one out of five males have been victims of sexual abuse before the age of eighteen. According to the American Academy of Experts in Traumatic Stress (AAETS), thirty percent of all male children and forty percent of females are molested in some way.

One of the effects of sexual abuse is that children abused at an early age often become hyper-sexualized and emotionally dysfunctional. Unfortunately, promiscuity and poor self-esteem are common reactions to sexual abuse early in life. Substance abuse is also a common outcome of sexual abuse. In fact, according to the AAETS, "specialists in the addiction field (alcohol, drugs, and eating disorders) estimate that up to ninety percent of their patients have a known history of some form of abuse."

I realized that God was leading me to identify my enemy. I was fighting the influence of what I had been exposed to. I was fighting the war over my soul and the war for my mind. This is real and needs to be confronted and dealt with, not swept under faith. God beckoned to me to expose the deepest parts of myself, face my abuser, challenge the lies that were left imprinted on me, and, eventually, begin to break the chains of my past that were attached to my heart, mind, and soul.

Today I challenge you to confront your enemy and start snapping chains. Your Father loves you too much to allow your faith-based practice to hide the freedom Christ died to give you.

Questions

Abuse was the cause of my hurt. What is yours?

Where are you hiding it (education, faith, success, religious activities, children, marriage, work)?

This is not a one-day experience. It is a continual conversation with the Father. If you need professional help uncovering and facing your issues, please seek a licensed professional.

Remember, life became better because of one who was not afraid to stand with passion and love for others! Let's go against the culture of selfishness with our actions, of self-care.

DAY TWENTY SIX – NEGATIVE CHATTER

Walking is a movement that advances you forward. Walking with God is to advance onward and forward with the perfect, omnipotent, omniscient originator and ruler of all. Can famine starve you? Can the desert kill you? Can enemies overtake you? Can the wilderness swallow you? What can stop your advancement to destiny? Your thoughts can!

According to an article in *Psychology Today*,[1] there are three main categories into which mental chatter falls: inferiority, love and approval, and control-seeking. If we gave God full control, accepted that the greatest love of all is not found in another human but rather the Father, and embraced God's word that we are a royal priesthood, would we solve the issue of negative chatter in our lives? Today we confront and kill the negative chatter that sows seeds of doubt in God and self. It stops you, sabotages relationships, causes self-doubt, and paralyzes. Tell the negative to flee. You are brave, you are powerful, you are capable, and YOU GOT THIS!

Consider that spontaneously occurring, negative thoughts are not random and do not stem from nowhere. Rather, they are rooted in deep-seated inferiority, a desire to be loved, and not feeling in control. Just as glossing over differences with one's spouse on essential issues can doom the relationship, glossing over negative thoughts by dealing with them on the surface, never digging deep to the root of these re-occuring thoughts can result in misery.

---

[1] https://www.psychologytoday.com/blog/sapient-nature/201310/how-negative-is-your-mental-chatter

Questions

Maintain an honest record of your thoughts as they occur during the week.

Does negativity dominate your thoughts?

In which category do they fit, inferiority, love, or control?

What does Scripture say about it? Use that scripture as your weapon to fight the lies and walk in truth.

DAY TWENTY SEVEN – Obedience

Obedience is obeying the lead and guidance of Jesus. You have free will and therefore the power and control to make choices. Jesus had a choice to make: allow mankind to die or sacrifice his life to save mankind. Jesus carried his cross and was crucified on that cross for you. You are *that* valuable to him. What is your cross? What is God requiring of you that seems impossible? For whom is God asking you to lay down your life that doesn't deserve it? Today, be encouraged that obedience to God is refining. It will not make sense to our flesh, but God always makes sense! Seek refuge in our Almighty God.

Meditation

"For I know the plans I have for you," declares the LORD, *"plans to prosper you and not to harm you, plans to give you hope and a future"* Jeremiah 19:11.

Jesus does not intend for us to follow a checklist to stay out of hell. Rather, he stresses a relationship with a loving, heavenly Father.

Questions

What is making the art and act of obedience difficult for you?

Is your way better than Jesus's plan for you?

What is controlling your struggle with obedience?

DAY TWENTY EIGHT – SNAKE BITE

The enemy will set you up in a dry place. He will send a snake uttering words dripping with honey and sweetness. Just like Eve, you will eat the fruit of seduction, betrayal, and death. How dangerous it is to know it's a serpent and yet thirst for its fruit! The sweetness arouses our senses and leaves a lasting impression that seems irresistible. It calls out to our needs, yearnings, desires, and fears. The serpent releases an intoxicating fragrance, which, once inhaled, can only be replaced by the aroma of deliverance, the fragrance of glory, the intoxicating fulfillment of God's love, the permanent healing of brokenness. It was the odor of brokenness that drew the snake to us. The counterfeit, temporary love of the snake is only a placebo and leads to death as it moves us from our postures, morals and commitments, drains our spirit of righteousness, and drops us wounded and depleted. Therefore, inhale and deeply take in God's true love so that you can exhale wholeness and change your aroma!

Meditation

Now the serpent was more crafty than any of the wild animals the Lord God had made. He said to the woman, "Did God really say, 'You must not eat from any tree in the garden'?" (Genesis 3:3 NIV)

Words enter the deepest, most delicate places in us and breed life or breed life to death.

Questions

What odor are you releasing?

What entices and draws you into its embrace?

What is the venom circulating in your mind that makes you think you need its nectar?

DAY TWENTY NINE – BOUND BY LOVE

L et love be without dissimulation. Abhor that which is evil and cleave to that which is good. Be kind and affectionate to one another in brotherly love; in honor preferring one another; not slothful in business; fervent in spirit; serving the Lord; Rejoicing in hope; patient in tribulation; continuing instant in prayer; If it be possible, as much as lieth in you, live peaceably with all men (Romans 12:9-12, 18 KJV).

I have been battling with my heart. I have been asking myself, "Why do I continue to love sharp edges? Am I a glutton for punishment? Is there something dysfunctional in me that holds on?" Despite experiencing all that I have, I continue choosing to love. The fight between my mind and my heart rages fiercely. My mind yells, "use logic and common-sense, let go!" My mind rehearses words like, "done," "removed," "finished," and "free." Am I living with the ghost of things past, clinging to a dangling hope that moves farther from my reach like a carrot swinging before me, snatched away as my hand grasps more of what has been? Why, heart, do you continually love sharp edges? You are bleeding from the wounds left on your emotions and self-worth. The Spirit weighs in, quoting the word of God, love counts no cost and it never let's go. It "bears all things, believes all things, hopes all things, and endures all things. Love never fails" (I Corinthians 13:7-8 NKJV).

My mind shouts, "Love never fails!? What?" My mind struggles to conceive of this ideal as hurt after hurt, disappointment after disappointment, loneliness, isolation, failed conversations, and denial flood my memory. Love has failed me since birth! My mind continues the fight. Perhaps your love, God, never fails! My reality has been one of faulty humans dropping and breaking people. I have been broken more times than I care to document. Abruptly interrupting my mind, my heart whispers sweetly, "your heart is made in my image. You love because I am love." You see, when Jesus enters and we give our lives, total selves, wills, and hearts completely over to Jesus, he changes us. He moves in and takes control. End this battle with a choice to trust. "My child. No, you are not insane! You are bound by love."

Meditation

My heart reflects my Father. I am His image. I am the *Imago Dei*.

Questions

What does "Imago Dei" mean? How does this affect my actions?

How do I protect myself from the opinions that are much like my old nature?

Who wins the battle most of the time, carnal mind or spirit?

Is there something greater happening in me as I submit?

How have the sharp edges of others sharpened me?

DAY THIRTY – DANCE LIKE EVERYONE IS WATCHING!

God is the choreographer of life. Seek Him daily to intently hear His divine music. Dance in tune, and on beat, with steps that enhance the partnership His choreography preaches. Learn to follow His lead as He spins, dips, and sometimes throws you, while never dropping you. Dance in the rain, sun, and cold. Dance on familiar ground and strange stages without losing trust in His grip. Learn to be lead by His sound. Enjoy the dance! Life is easier when your dance is divinely orchestrated.

Meditation

Dancing is a perpendicular expression of a horizontal desire. - George Bernard Shaw.

My youngest daughter, Aniyah Faith, deduced that this quote can be interpreted as "dance tells the story of connection". I concur.

Questions

What does this quote mean to you?

How is your dance?

Is there struggle and hesitation?

Are you leading or following?

Is it telling of your connection with the father?

DAY THIRTY-ONE – Divine Thought

I was walking down the street when a thought popped into my consciousness that was not my own. The thought played a statement for me that my husband, Greg, has always said, but that I had never really heard. Simply put, I was not looking for what he was giving me. I was looking for something else from him to soothe a wound he did not cause. In fact, I spent most of my marriage expecting him, along with God, to heal the wounds inflicted by my mother. But God needs no help. God wants no help. God wants all the glory and honor of your wholeness. That wholeness happens through the power of His voice. This book is about His voice and how to seek, hear, live by, and be made whole because of it. With each divine thought, I am raised from where I am laying down and stand in an upright position.

For many Mothers Days, my husband honored me by saying, "I chose the right woman to be the mother of my children." You may understand the power of that statement right away. Sadly, I did not hear it for fifteen years! I wanted and needed to hear from him that I am enough, beautiful, and loved. Do you see the problem with that? I wanted him to tell me all the things that God was already telling me, but it was not enough from God. I wanted Greg to affirm me. After years of praying and hiding behind my prayer life for comfort, God pulled me out of hiding to face the pain of the mental abuse. My mother never affirmed me, she broke me down with words that were intended to last a lifetime. The little girl, arrested in time, still seeks affirmation. I do believe that a healthy partnership of a husband and wife affirms. But what I desired was not healthy. Greg would have needed to constantly feed me the drug of affirmation because affirmation was not going to fix the deep-rooted problem. He could not break the chains on my heart and mind that were placed there by the damaging words sown in me as a child. Greg's statement contradicts statistical outcomes for people with a past like mine. Me, the "right mother?" What do I know about being a mother?

My mother made me sleep on the bathroom floor and beat me with a bat. On this day and through that thought, the divine voice of God revealed that, for years, Greg was giving me the highest honor and greatest compliment I had ever received. What he was confirming for me is that I overcame my predicted outcome. It took me fifteen years to hear and truly understand that. What are you looking and listening for that will not fix your core issue, but rather will give you instant, temporary gratification that you will need over and over again? I nudge you to seek God and listen for divine thoughts. Be made whole.

Meditation

Call to me and I will answer you and tell you great and unsearchable things you do not know (Jeremiah 33:3 NIV).

Questions

Is that which you desire from relationships healthy or instant gratification?

Are you baked macaroni and cheese or Kraft™ macaroni and cheese?

Are you willing to bake for a while to be the best version of yourself? It will get hot!

DAY THIRTY-TWO – MIND GAMES

When will I be able to write something different? When will I feel normal? What is normal? Am I normal? (I don't think so). Am I ruled by my inner enemy who desires to use my need to fuel an insatiable self-destruction? Am I fooled by my self-awareness? Am I convincing myself that deserving and wanting more warrants my behavior? If a cat stops chasing its tail, did it quit or give in? And if it catches its tail, will it hurt itself by its own bite? The problem is the unknown. How do I cease chasing my emotional need? Do my horrific actions have a simple reason? Or did I just want to stop chasing, if only for a moment to have my emotional need met? Ultimately hurting myself. There are so many reasons and affects. God, I needed to step out of "me," yet doing so injured "me." After all, it was "me" that made the choice. "Me" also made promises without fully understanding "me."

I am exposing the mind's interwinding of truth, justification, and lies. This is tiring and will most likely lead to bad decisions, self-harm, and mental anguish. When chasing the whys of your appetite overwhelms you, regroup and elect to chase the author of all truth. Stop retreating with scattered thoughts and mind games. Instead, hibernate and stabilize yourself in He who is constant, proven, and sure.

Meditation

Finally, brethren, whatsoever things are true, whatsoever things are honest, whatsoever things are just, whatsoever things are pure, whatsoever things are lovely, whatsoever things are of good report; if there be any virtue, and if there be any praise, think on these things (Philippians 4:8 KJV).

Do not get caught up in your mind. Remember that the mind is the battle ground and the enemy loves nothing more than to use your mind against you so that you self-destruct.

Questions

What thoughts do you battle?

Do they sound like that which God says about you?

Are they sabotaging thoughts?

DAY THIRTY-THREE – PERFECT LOVE
IS FOUND AT THE CROSS

The cross was offensive to me until I came to it. When was the last time you came to the cross?

At the cross, we see our ugly reflection of sin transformed into the beauty of love. The truth of our need for The Father is inescapable as we face the spotless image before us. Giving ourselves completely is an act of sacrifice that is rarely made. What does it mean to sacrifice and take up your cross?

EPILOGUE

Through the pages of this book, Jesus has been calling you to himself and to a higher dwelling in him. Jesus wants you to be as fanatically humble, sensitive, understanding, and generous as he is. Jesus is gently saying, "knowing, loving, resembling, and serving me must become the supreme passion of your life. Everything else comes second. Sometimes it will seem as though following Jesus is leading you places you do not understand and to where the only way seems like it will crush you. But do not go backwards and do not turn left or right. Jesus Christ's kingship will not crush you. He was crushed for you! Live free!

Thank you for joining me on the journey.

ABOUT THE AUTHOR

Nitisha Springer-Moore is a survivor of physical, mental, and sexual abuse and lung cancer. With this book, *A.M. Conversations with the Father,* she is making her debut as an author, sharing her journey to healing and wholeness through prayer with her transparent style.

She is an ordained minister and serves her community as a Community Development Manager for the American Cancer Society, a sought-after speaker, and spiritual advisor and mentor. She and her husband of seventeen years, Greg, demonstrate humanitarian qualities and feel that their family is called to service. Nitisha and Greg are the parents of two young-adult daughters and they reside in the Bronx in New York City.

Find out more about Nitisha at www.facebook.com/nmoore0927

Made in the USA
Middletown, DE
29 October 2020